THE PERSEVERANCE

Raymond Antrobus was born in Hackney, London to an English mother and Jamaican father. He is the recipient of fellowships from Cave Canem, Complete Works III and Jerwood Compton Poetry. He is one of the world's first recipients of an MA in Spoken Word Education from Goldsmiths, University of London. Raymond is a founding member of Chill Pill and the Keats House Poets Forum. He has had multiple residencies in deaf and hearing schools around London, as well as Pupil Referral Units. In 2018 he was awarded the Geoffrey Dearmer Award by the Poetry Society (judged by Ocean Vuong). Raymond currently lives in London and spends most his time working nationally and internationally as a freelance poet and teacher.

ALSO BY RAYMOND ANTROBUS

POETRY PAMPHLETS

To Sweeten Bitter (Out-Spoken Press, 2017)
Shapes & Disfigurements Of Raymond Antrobus
  (Burning Eye Books, 2012)

The Perseverance

Raymond Antrobus

Penned in the Margins
LONDON

PUBLISHED BY PENNED IN THE MARGINS
Toynbee Studios, 28 Commercial Street, London E1 6AB
www.pennedinthemargins.co.uk

The right of Raymond Antrobus to be identified as the author of this work has been asserted by him in accordance with Section 77 of the Copyright, Designs and Patent Act 1988.

First published 2018

Printed in the United Kingdom by TJ International

ISBN
978-1-908058-5-22

CONTENTS

ACKNOWLEDGEMENTS

Thanks to the editors at the following publications, where some of these poems were published previously, often in earlier versions: *POETRY, Poetry Review, The Deaf Poets Society, Magma, The Rialto, Wildness, Modern Poetry in Translation, Ten: Poets of the New Generation* (Bloodaxe Books), *The Mighty Stream, Filigree, Stairs and Whispers, And Other Poems, International Literature Showcase, New Statesman.*

I am grateful for support from Arts Council England, Sarah Sanders and Sharmilla Beezmohun at Speaking Volumes, Jerwood Compton Poetry Fellowship, Complete Works III, Cave Canem, Hannah Lowe, Shira Erlichman, Tom Chivers, my mother, my sister and Tabitha. The Austin family who gave me a place to stay in New Orleans, where I finished the manuscript. Malika Booker, Jacob Sam-La Rose, Nick Makoha, Peter Kahn.

Big up Renata, Ruth and all the NHS speech and language therapists I've had over the years. Big up Miss Mukasa, Miss Walker and Miss Willis, the English and support teachers at Blanche Neville Deaf School who helped me develop language and a D/deaf identity in the hearing world. I am me because you are you.

The
Perseverance

'There is no telling what language is
inside the body'
ROBIN COSTE LEWIS

Echo

My ear amps whistle as if singing
to Echo, Goddess of Noise,
the ravelled knot of tongues,
of blaring birds, consonant crumbs
of dull doorbells, sounds swamped
in my misty hearing aid tubes.
Gaudí believed in holy sound
and built a cathedral to contain it,
pulling hearing men from their knees
as though Deafness is a kind of Atheism.
Who would turn down God?
Even though I have not heard
the golden decibel of angels,
I have been living in a noiseless
palace where the doorbell is pulsating
light and I am able to answer.

What?

A word that keeps looking
in mirrors, in love
with its own volume.

What?

I am a one-word question,
a one-man
patience test.

What?

What language
would we speak
without ears?

What?

Is paradise
a world where
I hear everything?

What?

How will my brain
know what to hold
if it has too many arms?

The day I clear out my dead father's flat,
I throw away boxes of moulding LPs:
Garvey, Malcolm X, Mandela speeches on vinyl.

I find a TDK cassette tape on the shelf.
The smudged green label reads *Raymond Speaking.*
I play the tape in his vintage cassette player

and hear my two-year-old voice chanting my name, Antrob,
and Dad's laughter crackling in the background,
not knowing I couldn't hear the word "bus"

and wouldn't until I got my hearing aids.
Now I sit here listening to the space of deafness —

Antrob, Antrob, Antrob.

'And if you don't catch nothing
then something wrong with your ears —
they been tuned to de wrong frequency.'
KEI MILLER

So maybe I belong to the universe
underwater, where all songs
are smeared wailings for Salacia,
Goddess of Salt Water, healer
of infected ears, which is what the doctor
thought I had, since deafness
did not run in the family
but came from nowhere;
so they syringed olive oil
and salt water, and we all waited
to see what would come out.

And no one knew what I was missing
until a doctor gave me a handful of Lego
and said to put a brick on the table
every time I heard a sound.
After the test I still held enough bricks
in my hand to build a house
and call it my sanctuary,
call it the reason I sat in saintly silence
during my grandfather's sermons when he preached
The Good News I only heard
as Babylon's babbling echoes.

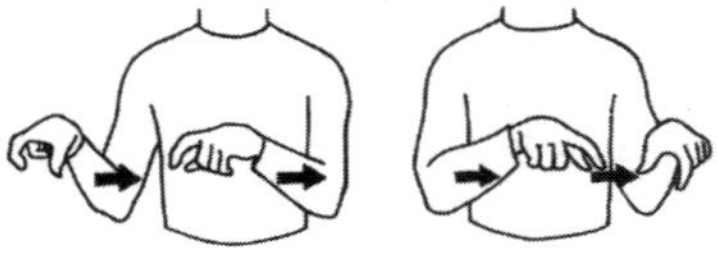

Aunt Beryl Meets Castro

listen listen, you know I
met Castro in Jamaica in
'77 mi work with
government under
Manley yessir you
should'da seen me up in
mi younger day mi give
Castro flowers
a blue warm warm
welcome to we
and mi know people who
nuh like it who say him
should stay smokin' in
him bush, our water and
wood nuh want problem
with dat blaze, but Castro,
him understan' the history
of dem who harm us, who
make the Caribbean a
kind of mix up mix up
pain. Me believe him

come to look us Black
people in the eye and say
we come from the same
madness but most people
nah wan brave no war and
mi understand dem, but
mi also know how we all
swallow different stones
on the same stony path.
Most dem on the Island
hear life in some Queen's
English voice but I was
tuned to dem real power
lines, I was picking up all
the signals. Some of dem
say, you know too much
yuh go mad, there a fear
of knowledge for the
power it bring and mi
understand dem just
trying to live and cruise
through life like raft
cruise Black River,
hunderstan'?

My Mother Remembers

serving Robert Plant, cheeky bugger,
tried to haggle my prices down.
I didn't care about velvet nothing.
I'm just out in snow on a Saturday market morning
trying to make rent and this is it:
when you're raised poor the world is touched
different, like you have to feel something, know it
with your hand. You need to know what is
worth what to who. I've served plonkers
in my time. That singer, Seal, tried to croon
my prices down. I was like, *no no, I'm one*
missed meal away from misery, mate!
I used to squat in abandoned factories,
go to jumble sales and come home to piece
together this cupboard, filling it with fabrics.
Then I met this wood sculptor, had these tree-trunk
forearms, said, *why not go to*
Camden Passage on Wednesday?
I had this van, made twenty-eight quid.

Look, everything I sold is listed in this notebook.
Fabrics, cleaned from your Great Gran's house.
Vintage. People always reach back to times
gone and that's what I'm saying,
people want to carry the past. Make it
fit them, make it say, *this is still us.*
I'd take sewn dresses made in the '20s.
Your Great Gran was a dressmaker,
you know, dresses carried her. I wore
this white and green thing to
her funeral. Sorry, guess everything
has its time. Are you ready to eat
or am I holding you up?

Jamaican British

after Aaron Samuels

Some people would deny that I'm Jamaican British.
Anglo nose. Hair straight. No way I can be Jamaican British.

They think I say I'm black when I say Jamaican British
but the English boys at school made me choose: Jamaican, British?

Half-caste, half mule, house slave — Jamaican British.
Light skin, straight male, privileged — Jamaican British.

Eat callaloo, plantain, jerk chicken — I'm Jamaican.
British don't know how to serve our dishes; they enslaved us.

In school I fought a boy in the lunch hall — Jamaican.
At home, told Dad, *I hate dem, all dem Jamaicans* — I'm British.

He laughed, said, *you cannot love sugar and hate your sweetness*,
took me straight to Jamaica — passport: British.

Cousins in Kingston called me Jah-English,
proud to have someone in their family — British.

Plantation lineage, World War service, how do I serve
    Jamaican British?
When knowing how to war is Jamaican British.

Ode to My Hair

When a black woman
with straightened hair
looks at you, says

nothing black about you,
do you rise like wild wheat
or a dark field of frightened strings?

For years I hide you under hats
and, still, cleanly you cling to my scalp,
conceding nothing

when they call you too soft,
too thin for the texture
of your own roots.

Look, the day is yellow Shea butter,
the night is my Jamaican cousin
saying *your skin and hair mean*

you're treated better than us,
the clippings of a hot razor
trailing the back of my neck.

Scissor away the voice of the barber
who charges more to cut
this thick tangle of Coolie

now you've grown a wildness,
trying to be my father's 'fro
to grow him out, to see him again.

The Perseverance

'Love is the man overstanding'
PETER TOSH

I wait outside THE PERSEVERANCE.
Just popping in here a minute.
I'd heard him say it many times before
like all kids with a drinking father,
watch him disappear
into smoke and laughter.

There is no such thing as too much laughter,
my father says, drinking in THE PERSEVERANCE
until everything disappears —
I'm outside counting minutes,
waiting for the man, my *father*
to finish his shot and take me home before

it gets dark. We've been here before,
no such thing as too much laughter
unless you're my mother without my father,

working weekends while THE PERSEVERANCE
spits him out for a minute.
He gives me 50p to make me disappear.

50p in my hand, I disappear
like a coin in a parking meter before
the time runs out. How many minutes
will I lose listening to the laughter
spilling from THE PERSEVERANCE
while strangers ask, *where is your father?*

I stare at the doors and say, *my father
is working.* Strangers who don't disappear
but hug me for my perseverance.
Dad said *this will be the last time* before,
while the TV spilled canned laughter,
us, on the sofa in his council flat, knowing any minute

the yams will boil, any minute,
I will eat again with my father,
who cooks and serves laughter
good as any Jamaican who disappeared
from the Island I tasted before

overstanding our heat and perseverance.

I still hear *popping in for a minute*, see him disappear.
We lose our fathers before we know it.
I am still outside THE PERSEVERANCE, listening for the laughter.

I Move Through London like a Hotep

What you need will come to you at the right time, says the
Tarot card I overturned at my friend Nathalie's house one
evening. I was wondering if she said something worth
hearing. *What?* I'm looking at her face and trying to read it,
not a clue what she said but I'll just say *yeah* and hope. Me,
Tabitha and her aunt are waffling in Waffle House by the
Mississippi River. Tabitha's aunt is all mumble. She either
said *do you want a pancake?* or *you look melancholic.* The less
I hear the bigger the swamp, so I smile and nod and my head
becomes a faint fog horn, a lost river. Why wasn't I asking
her to microphone? When you tell someone you read lips
you become a mysterious captain. You watch their brains
navigate channels with BSL interpreters in the corner of
night-time TV. Sometimes it's hard to get back the smooth
sailing and you go down with the whole conversation. I'm a
haze of broken jars, a purple bucket and only I know there's
a hole in it. On Twitter @justnoxy tweets, *I can't watch TV /
movies / without subtitles. It's just too hard to follow. I'm sitting
there pretending and it's just not worth it.* I tweet back, *you not*

being able to follow is not your failure and it's weird, giving the advice you need to someone else, as weird as thinking my American friend said, *I move through London like a Hotep* when she actually said, *I'm used to London life with no sales tax*. Deanna (my friend who owns crystals and believes in multiple moons) says I should write about my mishearings, she thinks it'll make a good book for her bathroom. I am still afraid I have grown up missing too much information. I think about that episode of *The Twilight Zone* where an old man walks around the city's bars selling bric-a brac from his suitcase, knowing what people need — scissors, a leaky pen, a bus ticket, combs. In the scene, music is playing loud, meaning if I were in that bar I would miss the mysticism while the old man's miracles make the barman say, *WOAH, this guy is from another planet!*

Sound Machine

'My mirth can laugh and talk, but cannot sing;
My grief finds harmonies in everything.'
JAMES THOMSON

And what comes out if it isn't the wires
Dad welds to his homemade sound system,
which I accidently knock loose
while he is recording Talk-Over dubs, killing
the bass, flattening the mood and his muses,
making Dad blow his fuses and beat me.
But it wasn't my fault; the things he made
could be undone so easily —
and we would keep losing connection.
But praise my Dad's mechanical hands.
Even though he couldn't fix my deafness
I still channel him. My sound system plays
on Father's Day in Manor Park Cemetery
where I find his grave, and for the first time
see his middle name, OSBERT, derived from Old English
meaning *God* and *bright*. Which may

have been a way to bleach him, darkest
of his five brothers, the only one sent away
from the country to live up-town
with his light skin aunt. She protected him
from police, who didn't believe he belonged
unless they heard his English,
which was smooth as some up-town roads.
His aunt loved him and taught him
to recite Wordsworth and Coleridge — rhythms
that wouldn't save him. He would become
Rasta and never tell a soul about the name
that undid his blackness. It is his grave
that tells me the name his black
body, even in death, could not move or mute.

Dear Hearing World

after Danez Smith

I have left Earth in search of sounder orbits,
a solar system where the space between
a star and a planet isn't empty. I have left
a white beard of noise in my place and many
of you won't know the difference. We are
indeed the same volume, all of us eventually fade.
I have left Earth in search of an audible God.
I do not trust the sound of yours.
You wouldn't recognise my grandmother's *Hallelujah*
if she had to sign it, you would have made her sit
on her hands and put a ruler in her mouth
as if measuring her distance from holy.
Take your God back, though his songs
are beautiful, they are not loud enough.

I want the fate of Lazarus for every deaf school
you've closed, every deaf child whose confidence
has gone to a silent grave, every BSL user
who has seen the annihilation of their language,
I want these ghosts to haunt your tongue-tied hands.
I have left Earth, I am equal parts sick of your
oh, I'm hard of hearing too, just because
you've been on an airplane or suffered head colds.
Your voice has always been the loudest sound in a room.

I call you out for refusing to acknowledge
sign language in classrooms, for assessing
deaf students on what they can't say
instead of what they can, we did not ask to be a part
of the hearing world, I can't hear my joints crack
but I can feel them. I am sick of sounding out your rules —
you tell me I breathe too loud and it's rude to make noise
when I eat, sent me to speech therapists, said I was speaking

a language of holes, I was pronouncing what I heard
but your judgment made my syllables disappear,
your magic master trick hearing world — drowning out the quiet,
bursting all speech bubbles in my graphic childhood,
you are glad to benefit from audio supremacy,
I tried, hearing people, I tried to love you, but you laughed
at my deaf grammar, I used commas not full stops
because everything I said kept running away,
I mulled over long paragraphs because I didn't know
what a *natural break* sounded like, ~~you erased~~
~~what could have always been poetry~~

You erased what could have always been poetry.
You taught me I was inferior to standard English expression —
I was a broken speaker, you were never a broken interpreter —
taught me my speech was dry for someone who should sound
like they're underwater. It took years to talk with a straight spine
and mute red marks on the coursework you assigned.

Deaf voices go missing like sound in space
and I have left earth to find them.

'Deaf School' by Ted Hughes

After Reading 'Deaf School' by the Mississippi River

No one wise calls the river *unaware* or *simple pools*;
no one wise says it *lacks a dimension*; no one wise
says its body is *removed from the vibration of air*.

The river is a quiet breath-taker, gargling mud.

Ted is *alert* and *simple*.
Ted *lacked* a *subtle wavering aura of sound*
and responses to Sound.

Ted lived through his eyes. But eye the colossal
currents from the bridge. Eye riverboats
ghosting a geography of fog.

Mississippi means *Big River,* named by French colonisers.
The natives laughed at their arrogant maps,
conquering wind and marking mist.

The mouth of the river laughs. A man in a wetsuit emerges,
pulls misty goggles over his head. *Couldn't see a thing.*
He breathes heavily. *My face was in darkness.*

No one heard him; the river drowned him out.

For Jesula Gelin, Vanessa Previl and Monique Vincent

When three deaf women
were found murdered,
their tongues cut out
for speaking sign language,

the papers called it
a savage ritualistic act —
but I think the world
should have gone silent,

should have heard the deaf
gather at Saint Vincent,
should have heard the quiet
march towards Port-au-Prince.

'The British government did not recognise British Sign Language until 2002'

BSL ZONE (DEAF HISTORY)

Before, all official languages
were oral. The Deaf were a colony
the hearing world ignored

and now, the irony, that the words *noise*
and *London* are the same sign in BSL.
It is getting so loud

audiologists are preparing
for the deafest generation
in heard history.

In Montego Bay, a sign
written on the outside walls
of the Christian deaf school says

Isiah 29:18 In that day the deaf shall hear

above a painting of a green hill paradise.
Harriott, the only Deaf teacher in the school,
tells me no one speaks sign well enough
to enter any visions of valleys.

My Dad never called me deaf,
even when he saw the audiogram.
He'd say, *you're limited,*
so you can turn the TV up.

He didn't mean to be cruel.
He was thinking about his friend
at school in Jamaica who stabbed
another boy's eardrums with pencils.

Dad never saw him in class again.
Maybe that's what he was afraid of;
that the deaf disappear, get carried away
bleeding from their ears.

Conversation with the Art Teacher
(a Translation Attempt)

*Shit and good my education. Hearing teachers not see potential.
This my confusion life, 90s hearing teachers not think I can
become artist because of deafness but funny thing, Deaf girl
does GCSE art in six months and go on to get degree. I have
proved many wrongs. I am costume designer, teacher, artist. At
school I said, "I want to be a costume designer." Teacher says,
"I can't." I can't? So harsh. My father, hearing, signs. Says I
can follow dream and lucky me, I did. Proving people wrong is
great but tiring. Was I born deaf? You asking lots of questions!
OK, yes, in Somaliland, I was about two, meningitis. Seven
other children in my hospital ward, all died. My father worked
around Europe and took me with him. English hospital saved
me. I still know some Somali sign. Wait, you write down what
I say, how? You know BSL has no grammar structure? How you
write me when I am visual? Me, into fashion, expression in
colour. How will someone reading this see my feeling?*

The Ghost of Laura Bridgeman Warns Helen Keller About Fame

They'll forget you, but not
   until men have sat close, touched
your hands, asked their questions.
     What is divinity? Eternity? Insouciance?

Your name will be scratched into reports
   naming you proof that those born
deaf or blind or both are worth
   an incapable God, a fragmented sermon.

They will want to know if "intelligence"
   has a hand shape. It took one man
called Dickens to open my story
   to the world and call it how he saw,

how he heard. Your danger is
   in his language. Don't let them twist
your silence — the ear and eye
   are at the seat of their perception.

We are centuries away from people
   believing our stories without
perversion, without pity. Their speech
   will never really find a way into us,

will always be the sound
   of our separation. Who is testing
God's hearing when you ask if my blood
   is dead? If I am dead, where is my thinking?

Beware of Alexander Graham Bell.
   Decibel is his word.
He never receives you. O Helen,
   don't trust what you cannot say yourself.

The Mechanism of Speech[*]

His tongue was too far forward

His tongue further back

His tongue too high, too low

His incorrect instrument

his difficult   power

to muscle

meaning

* Lectures delivered before the American Association to Promote the Teaching of Speech to the Deaf by Alexander Graham Bell. An erasure.

Doctor Marigold Re-evaluated

'If a written word can stand for an idea as well as a spoken word can,
the same may be said of a signed word'
HARLAN LANE

My BSL teacher taught me about affirmation and negation,
saying, in sign: *if you are crying and someone asks, "are you
crying?" you must answer with a smile and nod to affirm, "yes,
crying."*

I thought about Charles Dickens. About everyone laughing
and crying in 1843 while he performed Doctor Marigold.
The story is of a Cheap Jack trader pushing his cart through
east London, who adopts a deaf girl called Sophy after
losing his own daughter, because grief never leaves, it just
changes shape. Dickens visited deaf schools, interviewed
the students before shaping his story.

So let's love that Sophy and Doctor Marigold invent their
own home signs. Let's love that Sophy goes to a deaf school,
learns to read. Let's laugh when two deaf people fall in love.

Let's laugh when Sophy writes a letter to Doctor Marigold *hoping the child is not born deaf.* Let's laugh at the people who hope their child is born with a *pretty voice.* Let's speak in the BSL word order — *sign you speak?* — while celebrating and rolling our eyes at the signature *sentimental ending.* It's said that as Dickens read in Whitechapel, hearing people cried in the street when Sophy spoke (an unexplained miracle).

I want my BSL teacher to sign to everyone in 1843, *are you crying?* I want everyone to smile and nod, *yes, crying.*

The Shame of Mable Gardiner Hubbards

'Where in literature are the deaf seen truly, with deafness just one condition of their lives, acting in concert, with deaf and hearing people, not living as isolates?'
    LYDIA HUNTLEY SIGOURNEY (poet & teacher, 1814)

I shrink at any reference to my disability,
leave dinner halls with table edge marks in my chest
from hours leaning in. I lock myself in ladies' rooms
to rest, away from noise, to not be the girl going gah gah.
To pass as normal I rehearse my listening in mirrors.
My lips move and I wait for the right time to nod. A nod
restores my civility. I burned to absorb every decibel.
Look, ladies with perfect responses. A child drops
a spoon and their ears know where it landed.
Breed out our deafness, sterilise the shame of our species.
I love the man who forgets I cannot hear,
who plays piano and recites Shakespeare.
Everything he does shakes the floor; his name is Bell.

Two Guns in the Sky for Daniel Harris

When Daniel Harris stepped out of his car
the policeman was waiting. Gun raised.

I use the past tense though this is irrelevant
in Daniel's language, which is sign.

Sign has no future or past; it is a present language.
You are never more present than when a gun

is pointed at you. What language says this
if not sign? But the police officer saw hands

waving in the air, fired and Daniel dropped
his hands, his chest bleeding out onto concrete

metres from his home. I am in Breukelen Coffee House
in New York, reading this news on my phone,

when a black policewoman walks in, two guns
on her hips, my friend next to me reading

the comments section: *Black Lives Matter.*
Now what could we sign or say out loud

when the last word I learned in ASL was *alive*?
Alive — both thumbs pointing at your lower abdominal,

index fingers pointing up like two guns in the sky.

To Sweeten Bitter

My father had four children
and three sugars in his coffee
and every birthday he bought me
a dictionary which got thicker
and thicker and because his word
is not dead I carry it like sugar

on a silver spoon
up the Mobay hills in Jamaica
past the flaked white walls
of plantation houses
past canefields and coconut trees
past the new crystal sugar factories.

I ask dictionary why we came here —
it said *nourish* so I sat with my aunt
on her balcony at the top
of Barnet Heights
and ate salt fish
and sweet potato

and watched women
leading their children
home from school.
As I ate I asked dictionary
what is difficult about love?
It opened on the word *grasp*

and I looked at my hand
holding this ivory knife
and thought about how hard it was
to accept my father
for who he was
and where he came from

how easy it is now to spill
sugar on the table before
it is poured into my cup.

I Want the Confidence of

Salvador Dali in a 1950s McDonald's advert,
of red gold and green ties
on shanty town dapper dandies, of Cuba Gooding Jr.
in a strip club shouting *SHOW ME THE MONEY,*
of the woman on her phone in the quiet coach,
of knowing you'll be seen and served,
that no one will cross the road when they see you,
the sun shining through the gaps in the buildings,
a glass ceiling in a restaurant
where knives and spoons wink,
a polite pint and a cheeky cigarette, tattoos
on the arms, trains that blur the whole city without delay.
I want the confidence of a coffee bean in the body,
a surface that doesn't need scratching;
I want to be fluent in confidence so large it speaks from its own sky.
At the airport I want my confidence to board
without investigations, to sit in foreign cafés
without a silver spoon in a teacup clinking
into sunken places, of someone named after a saint,

of Matthew the deaf footballer who couldn't hear
to pass the ball, but still ran the pitch,
of leather jackets and the teeth
of hot combs, rollin' roadmen and rubber.
I don't want my confidence to lie;
it has to mean helium balloons in any shape or colour,
has to mean rubber tree in rain; make it
my sister leaving home for university, my finally sober father,
my mother becoming a circus clown.
There is such a thing as a key confidently cut
that accepts the locks it doesn't fit.
Call it a boy busking on the canal path singing
to no one but the bridges
and the black water under them.

After Being Called a Fucking Foreigner in London Fields

Because Dad slapped me
every time I fell into the metal railings
besides the swings, I was the first
in school to cycle without
training wheels. Dad's style
of discipline didn't check
for blood, just picked
me up with one hand,
red BMX in the other, his face
a fist, *come, come,*
pushed me along as I tried
to breathe and balance
the threat of a crash or
punch. A presence I feel in my chest
twenty-five years later walking
on the cycle path in the same park.
I keep my father's words, *violence
is always a failure*, so I don't

swing into the man's pale
bag-face when he throws
his arms up to fight me.
The truth is I'm not
a fist fighter. I'm all heart,
no technique. Last fought
at sixteen. Broke
two fingers and fractured
my wrist after a bad
swing, my boys bursting to see
a rumble, shouting, *breathe breathe breathe,*
which is also what my anger
counsellor said when I punched
the wall in her office but seriously —
who gets into fights in their thirties?
Nowadays, instead of violence,
I write until everything goes
quiet. No one can tell me
anything about this radiance.
I'm riding like a boy
on his red BMX — I see myself
turning off the path, racing past
the metal railings, the empty swings.

Closure

Because you stabbed me in the leg in Hackney Community College Library when I was seventeen over a computer, I wonder what else you would have opened me for?

—— —— —— —— —— —— —— —— —— —— —— —— —— —— —— ——

Nike Airs? A Nokia? A hot air balloon ride? Would you have opened me to run towards a Kenyan river?

—— —— —— —— —— —— —— —— —— —— —— —— —— —— —— ——

I forgive you for my twenty-one stitches; this scar is how I talk to you.

—— —— —— —— —— —— —— —— —— —— —— —— —— —— —— ——

We were boys, we were lost, we were worthy of space. It took me an age to learn there are men in the world who aren't here to hurt us. There is no knife I want to open you with. Keep all your blood.

—— —— —— —— —— —— —— —— —— —— —— —— —— —— —— ——

There is no kingdom to protect, these gates are open. I bring you food. Sit near the leg I couldn't move after the paramedics stapled it closed, while I pass you a plate of plantain.

—— —— —— —— —— —— —— —— —— —— —— —— —— —— —— ——

Laugh when you find out you knew my cousins, or our grandfathers arrived on the same boat, or worked in the same factories, denied the same rooms.

—— —— —— —— —— —— —— —— —— —— —— —— —— —— —— ——

Open your ground when we learn that the Jamaican man by the corner shop called us both *Little Springs*.

Maybe I Could Love a Man

I think to myself,
sitting with cousin Shaun in the Spanish Hotel

eating red snapper and rice and peas as Shaun says,
you talk about your father a lot, but I wasn't

talking about my father, I was talking about the host
on Smile Jamaica who said to me on live TV,

if you've never lived in Jamaica you're not Jamaican.
I said, *my father born here, he brought me back every year*

wanting to keep something of his home in me,
and the host sneered. I imagine my father laughing

at all the TVs in heaven. He knew this kind of question,
being gone ten years; people said, *you from foreign now.*

Cousin Shaun lifts his glass of rum, says, *why does anyone*
try to change who their fathers are. Later, it is enough

for me to sit with Uncle Barry as he tells me in bravado
about the windows he bricked, thrown out of pubs

for standing ground against the National Front. His name
for my father was 'Bruck', *because man always ready*

to bruck up tings, but I know my Uncle is just trying
to say, *I miss him.* Look what toughness does

to the men we love, me and Shaun are both trying to hold them.
But if our fathers could see us, sitting

in this hotel, they would laugh, not knowing
what else to do. But I walk away knowing

there are people here that remember my father,
people here who know who I am, who say

our grandfathers used to sit on that hill
and slaughter goats, while our fathers held

babies and their drinks, waving goodbye
to the people on Birch Hill who are and are not us.

Samantha*

What the Devil Said

Some believe I took Samantha's voice
at the moment she fell on these steps
in her council block, that I snatched
sounds from Samantha's world
like a collector of voice boxes.

According to her mother
I am like Samantha's father —
still somewhere behind her daughter,
on her shoulders, in her eyes,
all these years squeezing her dead tongue.

I'll watch what fires fester.
Look, Samantha knows who I am.
Before her hearing was knocked out
I appeared in tales her mother spun,
taking the form of a spider.

Her mother dreams of webs —
her daughter's voice held in my cords.
She tries to tear them like wires from walls;
she wails and wails with strain and scripture
but the web is a silk spell that won't break.

* These poems are based on an interview I conducted with a Deaf Jamaican woman about her arrival in England. I am honoured to have been given permission to write and share her story.

What Samantha Said

Sign is my home, a comfortable home
with only a few rooms I can share.

No one has told my mother the deaf have language.
No one she knows knows how to say this.

She knows fire is a God that won't stop shouting.
She knows that Job did not charge God for the life he lost.

I know the deaf are not lost
but they are certainly abandoned.

What Samantha's Mother Said

One night a woman at Bible study asks Samantha's mother,
why yuh daughter nuh speak, she ghost?

Samantha's mother swore
this was the moment the Devil's hand

appeared from behind the book, black and burnt,
covering Samantha's unmoveable mouth.

The Revivalists

The Revivalists congregate,
speaking in tongues to language

the Devil out of their imaginations.
A preacher in a suit ironed white

approaches the altar.
Staring into the pews, he points

at Samantha's silence and bellows,
who dare take their ears away from our Lord?

What Samantha's Father Said

Samantha's voice never returns but I do.
I see loneliness all over her like measles.

I bought her two rabbits. I mean, *who teaches us
more than the beasts of the earth?*

I see her sit in her room by the wide window,
stroking their ears, smiling at their twitches.

What Samantha's Sign Teacher Said

All good words in sign are said with the thumb —
useful, handsome, helpful.

These are the words I give Samantha
when her mother stands in my office shouting,

*if the Devil hasn't got my chile's voice
you make her speak!*

What Samantha Said at the End

We visited my mother after years estranged.

I heard her voice in bits, singing in the hospital.

Morning has bro n like the fi t morning

She had no teeth, her face looked chewed.

Black ird ha   poken like the fir   bird

She sounded rubbed away
but she still had an organ in her voice.

Pra   for the inging

I felt it vibrate under our feet as she hymned.

aise for the morning

She'd forgotten everything except God
and the fact she loves her daughter.

Praise for them pringing fre   rom the world.

Dementia had slowly removed
the Devil's hands from her ears.

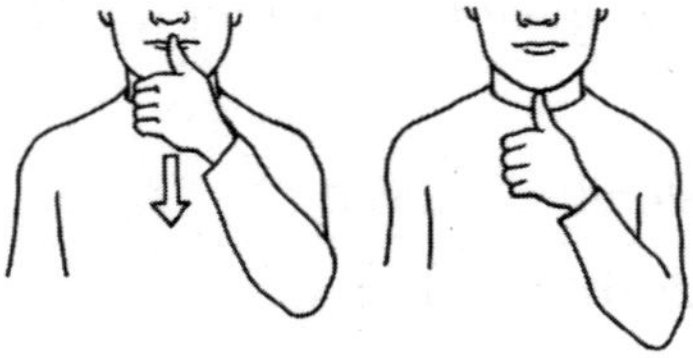

Thinking of Dad's Dick

after Wayne Holloway-Smith

The way it slipped out his trousers
like a horse's tongue, the way he'd shake it
after pissing, how wide
and long it was. I never thought I'd compete.
Funny to thank him for this now,
how he didn't really have secrets, was open
about his three children with three different women,
how he ran from them. He told me he'd had sex
with 48 women in his life, said his first week in London
a woman sucked his dick on the top floor of a night bus.
He never held back details. He knew he wouldn't live
to see me grown. I know that now. He had to give,
while he could, the length of his life to me.

Miami Airport

why didn't you answer me back there?

you know how loud these things are on my waist?

you don't look deaf?
>>> can you prove it?
>>>>> do you know sign language?
> I.D.?
>>> why didn't I see anyone that looked like you
>>>> when I was in England?

why were you in Africa?

why don't you look like a teacher?

who are these photos of?

is this your girlfriend?

why doesn't she look English?

        what was the address you stayed at?

    what is the colour
        of the bag you checked in?

what was your address again?

        is that where we're going to find dope?

    why are you checking your phone?
        can I take your fingerprints?
why are your palms sweating?

        you always look this lost?

    why did you tell me your bag was red?

how did it change colour?

    what colour are your eyes?

how much dope will I find in your bag?

why isn't there dope in your bag?

why did you confuse me?

why did you act strange when there was nothing on you?

would you believe
what I've seen in the bags of people like you?

you think you're going
to go free?

what did you not hear?

His Heart

turned against him in a chicken shop
he said, *my heart is falling out*

as he slipped into dreams
of his mother in Jamaica

he came through in hospital, longing
for that woman, dead twenty years

his son visits and they spend
half an hour holding hands

there is a needle in his arm
and blood in his colostomy bag

he asks the nurse if he can go to the post office
to buy his daughter a postcard

but forgiveness does not
have an address

Madge is the first girl he kissed in Jamaica
white floral dress, scent of thyme and summer

she visits his hospital dreams
Madge is not the nurse who dissolves

painkillers in his water
he does not drink with his eyes open

his son turns on the radio
it is *A Rainy Night In Georgia*

his son, a blur
on a wooden chair

Dementia

'black with widening amnesia'
DEREK WALCOTT

When his sleeping face
was a scrunched tissue,
wet with babbling,

you came, unravelling a joy,
making him euphoric, dribbling
from his mouth —

you simplified a complicated man,
swallowed his past
until your breath was
warm as Caribbean
concrete —

O tender syndrome
steady in his greying eyes,
fading song
in his grand dancehall,

if you must,
do your gentle magic,
but make me unafraid
of what is

disappearing.

Happy Birthday Moon

Dad reads aloud. I follow his finger across the page.
Sometimes his finger moves past words, tracing white space.
He makes the Moon say something new every night
to his deaf son who slurs his speech.

Sometimes his finger moves past words, tracing white space.
Tonight he gives the Moon my name, but I can't say it,
his deaf son who slurs his speech.
Dad taps the page, says, *try again.*

Tonight he gives the Moon my name, but I can't say it.
I say *Rain-nan Akabok*. He laughs.
Dad taps the page, says, *try again,*
but I like making him laugh. I say my mistake again.

I say *Rain-nan Akabok*. He laughs,
says, *Raymond you're something else.*
I like making him laugh. I say my mistake again.
Rain-nan Akabok. What else will help us?

He says, *Raymond you're something else.*
I'd like to be the Moon, the bear, even the rain.
Rain-nan Akabok, what else will help us
hear each other, really hear each other?

I'd like to be the Moon, the bear, even the rain.
Dad makes the Moon say something new every night
and we hear each other, really hear each other.
As Dad reads aloud, I follow his finger across the page.

NOTES

'Echo': Kei Miller's line appears in his collection, *Light Song Of Light* (Carcanet, 2010). There is an essay about this poem published on poetryfoundation.org, titled 'Echo, A Deaf Sequence'. Thanks to Don Share for featuring this poem on The Poetry Magazine Podcast, March 6th 2017.

'Jamaican British': Inspired by Aaron Samuels' poem 'Broken Ghazal', in *The BreakBeat Poets* (Haymarket Books, 2015).

'The Perseverance': The Perseverance is the pub on Broadway Market my Dad used to drink in. 'Love is the man overstanding' is from Peter Tosh's 'Where You Going To Run' which appears on *Mama Africa* (EMI, 1983). This poem is a Sestina.

'I Move Through London Like A Hotep: References *The Twilight Zone* episode, 'What You Need' (season 1, episode 12).

'Sound Machine': James Thomson's line is from 'Two Sonnets', originally written in 1730 and reprinted in Don Patterson's *Sonnets 101* (Faber, 2012).

'Dear Hearing World': Parts of this poem are riffs and remixes of lines from *Dear White America* by Danez Smith (Chatto/Greywolf, 2012). Deaf actress Vilma Jackson performs a BSL version of this poem in a short film produced by Adam Docker at Red Earth Studios.

'Deaf School by Ted Hughes': Originally published in *The Quiet Ear: Deafness in Literature : An Anthology*, edited by Brian Grant (Faber, 1988). Hughes admits that this poem was written quickly in his notebook after visiting a deaf school in London.

'After Reading Deaf School by the Mississippi River': This poem would not exist without inspiration from Shira Erlichman and the poem 'The Moon Is Trans' by Joshua Jennifer Espinoza.

'For Jesula Gelin, Vanessa Previl and Monique Vincent': This poem would not exist without the article, 'Killing of deaf Haitian women highlights community's vulnerability' in the *Jamaica Observer*, which I read while in Kingston visiting family in April 2016.

'Conversation with the Art Teacher (a Translation Attempt)': With thanks to Naimo Duale and Oaklodge Deaf School.

'The Ghost of Laura Bridgeman Warns Helen Keller About Fame': This poem would not exist without the academic writing of Jennifer Esmail (*Reading Victorian Deafness*) at the University of Toronto, Gerald Shea (*Language Of Light*) at Yale University and Laurent Clerc (*Autobiography*, Gallaudet University, 1817). Laura Bridgeman was a Deaf-Blind student at the Blind Asylum in Boston, who was made famous after Charles Dickens took an interest in her. You can read transcripts in Dickens' *American Notes For General Circulation, Jan – June 1842*, in which some of Bridgeman's answers are lifted and put into this poem.

'The Mechanism of Speech': Alexander Graham Bell, famous for inventing the telephone, spent the latter part of his life giving lectures around America and Europe promoting oralism to teachers of the deaf as well as hearing families with deaf children. His lectures were geared towards proving all deaf people could access speech if they are not encouraged to use sign language. He used famous names of his time such as Helen Keller as proof of this, but his case studies were later proved to be either flawed or fraudulent. Interestingly enough, both Bell's wife and mother were deaf. In *Reading Victorian Deafness*, Jennifer Esmail says 'the root of oppression for deaf people is being forced to speak'.

'Doctor Marigold Re-evaluated': 'Doctor Marigold' is a short story written by Charles Dickens. This poem would not exist without Jennifer Esmail's *Reading Victorian Deafness* and my BSL level 2 teacher, Debora who teaches for the BSL organisation in London, Remark!

'The Shame of Mable Gardiner Hubbards': Mable was profoundly deaf from five years old and married Graham Alexander Bell. Her name then changed to Mable Bell. Laurent Clerc, one of the first Deaf teachers at Gallaudet University, quotes her diary in his autobiography, in which she admits, 'I hate the deaf and anyone who teaches them'.

'Two Guns in the Sky for Daniel Harris': Written after reading the CNN article, 'After trooper kills deaf man, North Carolina family seeks answers' in August 2016. The case was dropped in January 2017 and no one was charged.

'Closure': Thanks to the NHS paramedics, nurses and doctors at Homerton Hospital, who stitched me up and saved my life. This poem would not exist without them and Caroline Bird.

'Maybe I Could Love a Man': References my father's ancestral land in Jamaica, Birch Hill and Patty Hill. Big love to cousin Dean, cousin Shaun, Uncle Barry, Alison and Hilary in Kingston.

'What Samantha Said': This sequence of seven poems exists thanks to a friend who wishes to be anonymous but who gave me the honour of sharing her story as a Deaf Jamaican woman who moved to London in the 1980s. The details of this story were gathered via face-to-face interviews using BSL and SSE (Sign Supported English). Samantha means "the one who hears", "God Heard" and "Listener" in Hebrew, Greek, Aramaic and English.

'Thinking Of Dad's Dick': This poem wouldn't exist without Wayne Holloway Smith sharing his poem sequence with me. His poem 'Dad's Dick' was originally published in *The Poetry Review*.

'Dementia': I cared for my father for two years while he was dying. Seriously, big up the carers of the world. Thanks also to the NHS nurses and to Halima; I couldn't have pushed through without you.

'Happy Birthday Moon': A pantoum inspired by Frank Asch's children's picturebook of the same title.

A note on the spelling of D/deaf

Thoughout the book, these poems use variations of big D and little d D/deaf. Big D Deaf people are those who are born Deaf and tend to learn sign before spoken language is acquired and regard their deafness as part of their identity and culture rather than as a disability.

Small d deaf people are often those who become deaf in later life, after they have acquired a spoken language. Their relationship with deafness is more medical than cultural.

FURTHER READING

Magma 69 (The Deaf Issue) edited by Lisa Kelly & Raymond Antrobus (2017)

Understanding Deaf Culture: In Search of Deafhood by Paddy Ladd (2003)

Seeing Voices by Oliver Sacks (2012)

When The Mind Hears: A History Of The Deaf by Harlan Lane (1994) ·

This book includes a spotify soundtrack; search 'The Perseverance' or log on to raymondantrobus.com.

The BSL and ASL illustrations are by Oliver Barrett (floatinglimb.com).